Clemons Van Forer's Freedom

Joshua Augustus Clemons

McPubKids
A Division of McClure Publishing, Inc.

Johusa Augustus Clemons Copyright © 2021 by McPubKids, a division of McClure Publishing, Inc.
1st Edition – ISBN: 978-1-7347595-9-4

Published in the United States by McClure Publishing, Inc. | Bloomingdale, Illinois | 800.659.4908

https://www.mcpubkids.com
books@mcpubkids.com

Illustrator: Lamont Wayne

Editor: Jennifer Petticolas
jlp7139@yahoo.com

Filed under Library of Congress Catalog Number: 2021922784

Clemons Van Forer's Freedom

Written by Joshua Augustus Clemons

Illustrations by Lamont Wayne

Acknowledgements

I want to thank Jennifer Lipford Petticolas. She is my Grandma. I thank my Grandma because she helped me edit; she helped me find an illustrator. She taught me about similes. She also taught me how to read. So, thank you!

I want to thank my other grandparents and great grandparents for loving and supporting me.

I want to thank my Mom. One day she told me to write a story. I wrote more and more. So, thank you, Mom!

I want to thank my dad for teaching me to love sports. He taught me how to play soccer!

I want to thank my Aunt Kish. She took me on my first movie date. She is teaching me about stocks. Thank you so much Aunt Kish for loving, supporting, and teaching me!

I also want to thank my teachers for making me write random stories in the mornings. As I rise to higher grades, I will write more stories.

Last, but not least, I want to thank you! I want to thank you for reading my book. You are great readers; I know you will also write good stories.

As John's mother walked into the dining room, she saw John jumping up and down around the dining room table like popcorn in a popcorn popper. "What are you so excited about?" she asked.

"I can't wait for Juneteenth," John said to his mother with joy.

"What are you going to do for Juneteenth?" his mother asked.

"I'm excited about a story I wrote," said John.

Smiling, John's mother asked, "Is your story about freedom for some of our people?"

John thought for awhile, then he said, "Yes and no."

Puzzled, his mother said, "I don't understand. What do you mean? What is it about?"

"I'll read it to you," said John!

He pulled a wrinkled sheet of paper out of his pocket. He put it on the table. He flattened it and began reading his story.

In 1839, there was an enslaved man named Clemons Van Forer. He was a hard worker. He wanted to be free. He dreamed of gathering his family together and escaping to freedom. He had heard stories about an enslaved man named Tice Davids escaping to freedom on something called the Underground Railroad. But until he could escape to freedom, he would enjoy the freedom he created on the plantation.

As an enslaved person, he faced many bad things
One bad thing was he feared his family might be
sold.

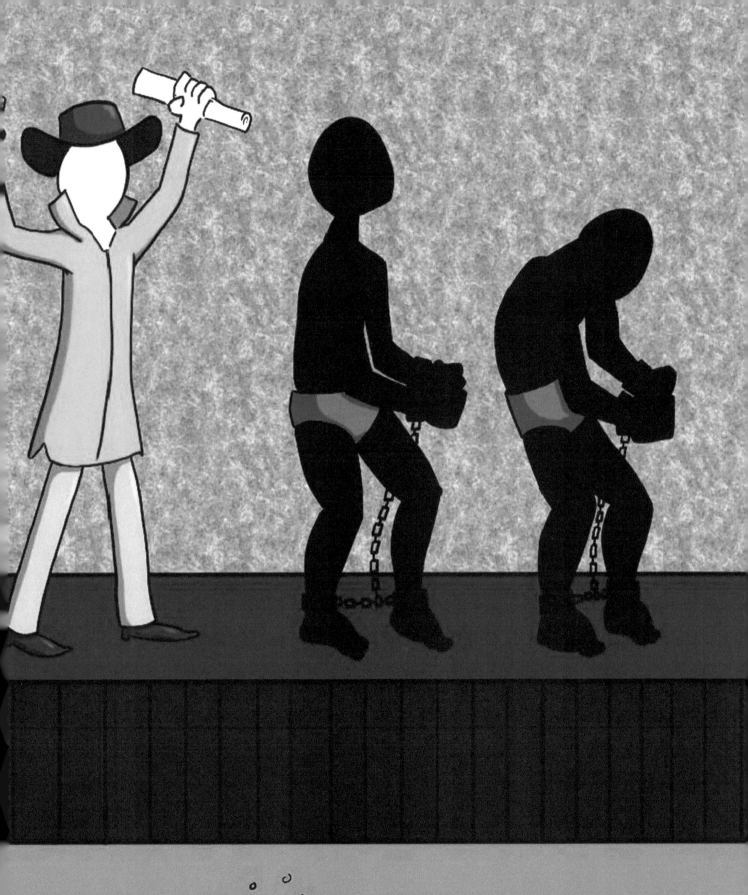

He saw many families separated and sold, never to see each other again.

Another bad thing for him was picking cotton. He picked cotton from sunrise till darkness of night.

By mid-day, the sun was beating down on him. The sun felt like fire on his skin. Sweat dripped from him. His fingers ached. They were tired and painful. He learned the things that made him cry also made him tough.

He loved his family very much. Clemons's wife was named Shaka. Shaka cleaned the big house. They had two boys and one girl. The girl's name was Mateia. She was nine years old. Mateia cleaned with her mother.

The boys were Rob and Larry. Rob was ten years old, and Larry was six years old. The boys' job was to feed the animals in the dirty barn.

As Clemons stood to wipe sweat from his forehead, he could see his cabin.

He could not wait to see his family at the end of the day. He felt freedom with his family.

When the family returned to their cabin, they were exhausted. Beside the door of the cabin there was a bucket of water. At the end of each day, before they entered the cabin, Clemons poured water over the heads of his wife and children. The water was a way of freeing them from another day of being enslaved Clemons said, "They may own us, but they don't own our spirit of love."

Clemons and his family entered their cabin where they had freedom until the sun rose the next morning.

lemons's family was his heart. His freedom!
heir hearts were filled with love for each other.

Looking up at his
mother, John said,
"The end!"

His mother winked.

"I love it! You did a great job! I am so proud of you!" His mother kissed the top of his head.

That night, before John went to bed, his mother stood outside his bedroom door and listened as her son prayed. She was proud but sad as she listened.

God, I am thankful that I am Black. Please forgive people who do not like me because I am Black. Please help me to face bad things with love in my heart. Amen."

Glossary

Juneteenth is June 19th. Although slavery had ended, it marked the end of slavery for enslaved people in Texas. On June 19, 1865, Galveston, Texas received word that slavery had ended when Abraham Lincoln signed Proclamation of Emancipation freeing enslaved people on September 22, 1862. President Joe Biden signed it as a national holiday on June 17, 2021.

The Underground Railroad was not a train railroad. The Underground Railroad was homes, churches, and businesses called stations. The people in these stations provided food and a place to hide for runaway enslaved people seeking freedom. People who helped enslaved people moved from one station to another were called conductors.

Tice Davids was an enslaved person from Kentucky. In 1831, he escaped from his owner crossing the Ohio River. His owner chased him in a rowboat, but Tice got to shore before his owner. When his owner got to shore, he could not find Tice. When the owner returned home, he told people that Tice Davids must have escaped by an underground railroad. It is believed, by some people, this is how the Underground Railroad got its name.

About the Author

 Joshua Augustus Clemons is eight years old; he is in the third grade. He lives in Virginia. Joshua enjoys writing and creating fictional stories. Not only does he love writing, Joshua loves sports. He loves to draw, sing, and dance.

What he loves most is spending time with his family, friends, and dogs, Josie and Nugget. Joshua strongly believes in prayer. He loves talking to God.

9 781734 7595